# Contents

# Introduction

This book will take you into the beautiful world of the rainforest. It describes each layer of the forest, from the tops of its tallest trees, down to the forest floor and rivers. You will find some of the amazing creatures that live in different parts of the forest.

Rainforests can be found all around the world, close to the equator. There are rainforests in Central and South America, the Congo, Madagascar and Southeast Asia.

All of the rainforests of the world are located around the equator. The equator is the invisible line stretching around the centre of the planet.

On each spread you will have to look for different objects in the main picture.

# Rainforest Overview

Rainforests grow near the equator, in places that are warm with lots of rain. The Amazon forest in South America is the largest rainforest – it is about 6.5 million square kilometres (2.5 million $m^2$). More plants and animals live there than any other place on Earth. There are four main areas in a rainforest: the emergent layer at the top, then the canopy, the understorey and the forest floor.

## Emergent layer

The tops of the biggest trees in the forest. They are filled with flowers and fruit.

## Canopy

A thick, leafy layer high above the forest floor. Most rainforest animals live here.

## Understorey

Many mammals, birds and insects live in this darker area under the canopy.

## Forest floor

Ferns and mosses grow here. Silent hunters hide in its dark shadows.

## Forest People

They build houses, hunt for food and live off whatever the rainforest can provide.

## The Riverbank

Tree roots spread out into the river. Giant otters, alligators and river plants live in the water.

# Life at the Top

The tallest trees in the rainforest push above the thick canopy layer of branches and leaves to reach sunlight. This gives them more space and light to grow.

These umbrella-shaped trees can be over 61 metres (200 feet) tall, but they have very shallow roots. When a tree falls, it smashes through the forest and creates a wide open space.

◀Black-headed squirrel monkey
These monkeys like eating spiders and frogs.

Can you find...?

▲Quetzal
A male quetzal's tail feathers can be over 1 metre (39 inches) long.

▲Hyacinth macaw
The hyacinth macaw is the largest of all parrots.

▲Male topaz hummingbird
This is one of the biggest hummingbirds.

◀Gouldian finch
These birds live off small insects and seeds.

▲Morpho butterfly
These beautiful blue butterflies can be the size of a dinner plate.

▲Amazilia dumerilii hummingbird
These birds feed mainly on nectar.

▲King vulture
This large vulture can fly for hours without landing.

▶Toucan
Toucans nest in tree holes. They use their large beaks to eat and to attract mates.

# The Understorey

Beneath the canopy is the darker understorey. This layer consists of tangled shrubs, young trees and vines.

The hot, damp conditions here are perfect for mosses and algae to grow. The darkness suits nocturnal animals, such as sloths. Birds and lizards feed off the insects that live in the understorey.

Can you find...?

**▲Orangutan**
These large apes like hanging around in the treetops. They live, eat and sleep there.

**▲Emperor tamarin**
This monkey eats insects, tree sap and fruit.

**▲Blue and gold macaw**
This noisy parrot eats nuts and fruit, just like the scarlet macaw.

**◀Three-toed sloth**
The world's slowest mammal, the sloth hangs upside down from branches.

◀Stag beetle
There are 1,200 kinds of stag beetle in the world.

▲Butterflies
There are many colourful butterflies in the rainforest.

▲Tree frog
There are over 800 kinds of tree frog. Their toe pads help them to climb.

▲Scarlet macaw
This colourful parrot nests in trees.

▶Green iguana
This lizard can use its tail to whip any predators.

Can you find...?

# In the Shade

Few plants grow in the dark, damp shade of the forest floor. Only mosses and ferns can survive in this endless gloom. But the dark open spaces make it ideal for hunting. There are many predators, such as jaguars and large snakes.

▲Jaguar
These big cats have a patterned coat that helps to 'camouflage' or hide them.

Emerald tree boa

These big snakes swallow their victims whole.

◀Capybara These guinea pig-like rodents can be over 1.3 metres (4 feet) long.

## ▶South American coati

These ring-tailed animals only live in the rainforests and jungles of South America.

## ▲White-tailed deer

These deer have a reddish-brown coat in spring and summer which turns grey-brown in autumn and winter.

## ▲Armadillo

These mammals have armour-like leathery scales. They have bad eyesight, so they rely on their nose to find food.

An opossum's large eyes and ears help it to detect approaching predators. These small animals 'play possum', or pretend to be dead, when in danger.

## ◀Woolly opossum

Can you find...?

# The Riverbank

▲Giant otter
Giant otters are rare now because they are hunted for their thick, glossy fur.

The roots and green shoots of many rainforest plants grow into thick, tangled clumps that line the riverbank. This damp, warm layer of the forest is home to many reptiles and amphibians (animals that live on land and in the water).

The alligators and giant otters that live here are good hunters and live mostly on fish. Seeds from the creepers, bushes and trees that grow in the riverbank soil add even more plants to the rainforest.

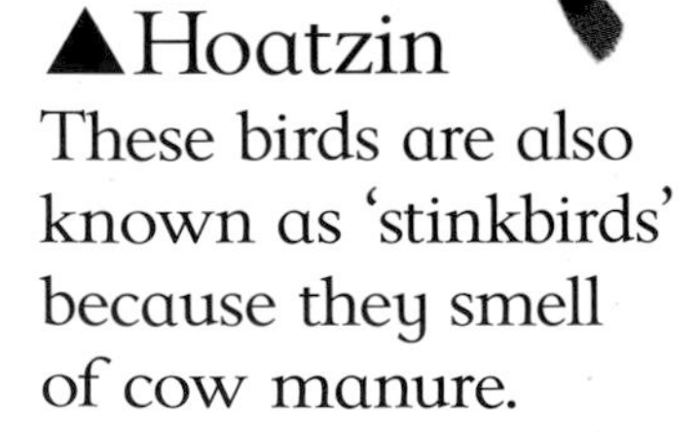

▲Hoatzin
These birds are also known as 'stinkbirds' because they smell of cow manure.

◀Alligator
American alligators are reptiles. They have between 74 and 80 teeth.

▶ Blue frog

Poisonous rainforest frogs are often brightly coloured to warn off predators.

▲ Vine

Plants that grow on the forest floor and climb towards the canopy.

▲ Fish

Over 1,500 species of fish live in the rainforest rivers. Piranha fish have razor-sharp teeth.

▼ Dragonfly

These insects can hover and fly forwards, backwards or sideways.

# Forest People

For centuries, rainforest people have lived in the forests. They rely on their surroundings for food, shelter and medicines. By using only what the forest provides they can conserve their forest home. They make simple dugout canoes from hollowed-out tree trunks and make blowpipes for hunting.

## Can you find...?

### Under threat
Old medicines cannot cure new diseases. Blowpipes are no match for bulldozers. Without money, rain forest people cannot fight development. Like their beautiful homeland, they are also under threat.

### ▲Thatched roofs
Roofs are made out of dried grass and reeds that have been tied together. This protects the forest people from the rain.

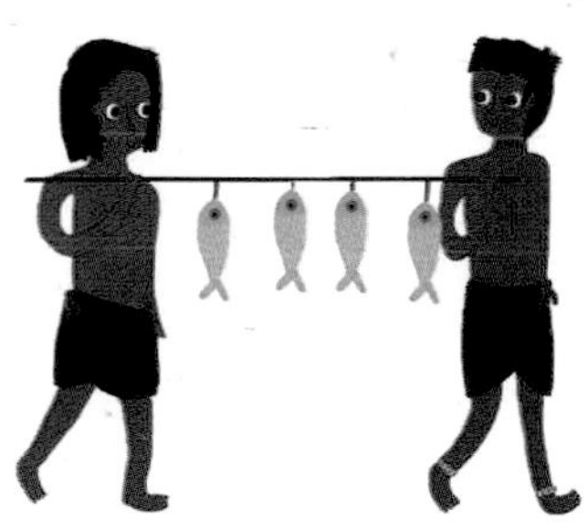

### ▲Fishing
Fish from the rainforest rivers provide food for the community.

### Farming
They build houses and grow crops in small areas of the forest. After a few years, they move on, allowing the forest to grow again.

# Destruction

Rainforests are disappearing. They are being cut down for their timber and to make space to build ranches, mines and plantations.

Once the trees are cut down, valuable soil gets washed away with the rainwater. This soil ends up choking the rivers and causing flooding. The soil left behind is not good for growing things.

## Can you find...?

### Deforestation

Cutting down huge areas of rainforest creates problems. Trees absorb the greenhouse gases that are making our planet heat up. Rainforests help to keep our planet safer. Without shelter from the trees, the forest soils dry out quickly in the sun. The land can turn into empty desert.

### Nutrients

Dead, decaying trees pass on nutrients to living trees. This helps them to grow better.

### Forest fires

Trees and plants in the rainforest are being burned down to clear the land for animals to be farmed. This is destroying the natural habitats of many forest species.

# Timeline

**55 million years ago**
The Amazon rainforest was formed.

**1500s AD**
Older civilisations may have lived in the Amazon rainforest before the arrival of European explorers in the 16th century.

**8,000 BC**
The first people to live in the Amazon rainforest arrived.

**1972**

The building of the Trans-Amazonian Highway began. This road was meant to join up many different states in Brazil. Large parts of the rainforest have been lost because of it.

**1960s**

Farms were built in the rainforest. To make space for them, thousands and thousands of trees were cut down and burned.

**1900s onwards**

Since the beginning of the last century, people have been trying to conserve and protect large areas of the rainforest and the people who live there.

# Quiz

1. Which monkey likes to eat spiders and frogs?
2. Which large bird can fly for hours without landing?
3. Which ape spends most of its time in the treetops?
4. What is the world's slowest mammal?
5. Which animal has a tough, leathery shell used as armour against predators?
6. Which creature can swallow its victims whole?
7. Which reptile has about 80 teeth?
8. Which animal is hunted for its thick, glossy fur?
9. What do rainforest people use to make roofs for their shelters?
10. What do rainforests help to absorb?

Answers:

1. Black-headed squirrel monkey
2. King Vulture
3. Orangutan
4. Three-toed sloth
5. Armadillo
6. Emerald Tree Boa
7. American alligator
8. Giant otter
9. Dried grasses and reeds
10. Greenhouse gases

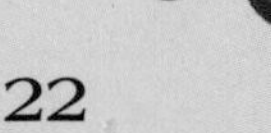

# Glossary

**Algae** Plants that usually live in the water and use sunlight to create their food.

**Blowpipe** A long tube used to fire a poisoned dart or arrow by blowing air into it. It is used as a weapon.

**Camouflage** A covering, like skin or fur, that blends in with the environment and disguises the animal.

**Canopy** The high up branches and thick foliage of the trees in a rainforest.

**Conservation** The attempts to protect the vegetation and wildlife on our planet so that it doesn't disappear.

**Equator** An imaginary line around the middle of the globe, between the North and South Poles.

**Moss** A type of plant that grows in damp environments and is usually green in colour.

**Nectar** A sugary liquid in flowers which attracts insects. Bees collect it to make honey in their hives.

**Nocturnal** Something, such as an animal or plant, that is most active at night.

**Nutrients** Substances that provide the energy that animals need to live.

**Species** A group of similar living things which are able to mate and reproduce.

**Thatch** A roof covering made from layers of dry straw, reeds or palm fronds.

**Timber** Wood that has been cut down and prepared for use in building or carpentry work.

# Index